RONALD SEARLE's
Big Fat Cat Book

RONALD SEARLE'S
Big Fat Cat Book

Little, Brown and Company – Boston – Toronto

First American edition published in 1982 by
Little, Brown and Company
34 Beacon Street, Boston, Massachusetts 02106

Library of Congress Catalog Card Number: 82 – 81345

This book was designed and produced by
The Rainbird Publishing Company Limited
40 Park Street, London W1Y 4DE

ISBN 0 316 77898 2

Photography by Rosmarie Nohr, Munich; Graham Bush,
London and André Chadefaux, Paris

Colour reproduction by Scanplus Limited, London
Printed and bound by W. S. Cowell Limited, Ipswich, England

Endpapers: Love Feast
Half title: The Messenger
Frontispiece: Family Photo
Title: Ragtime
Facing page: The Guru

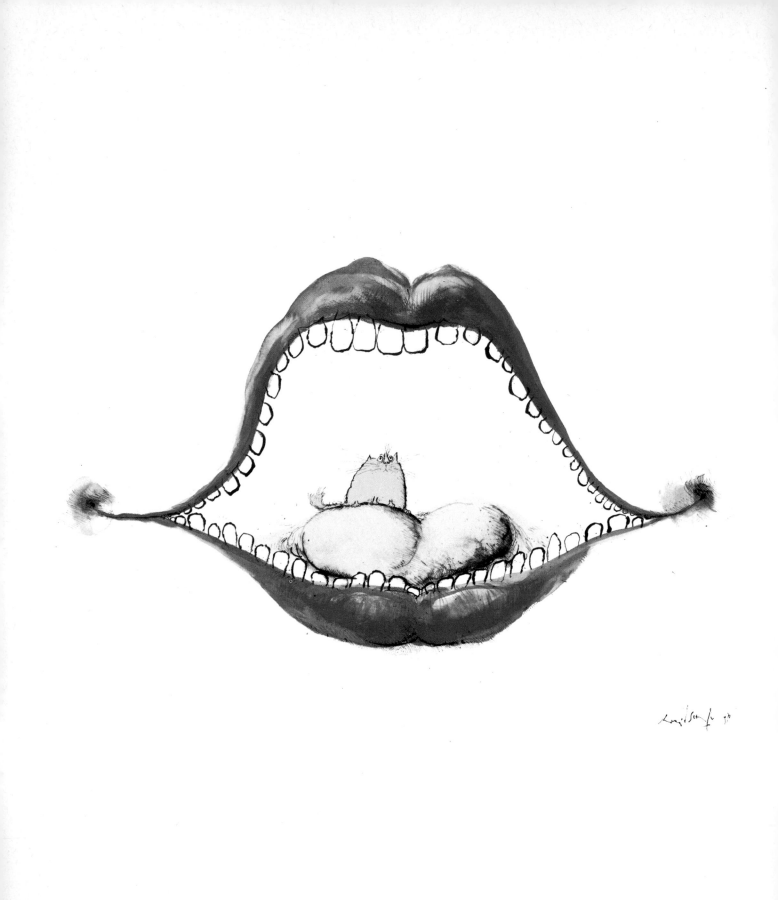

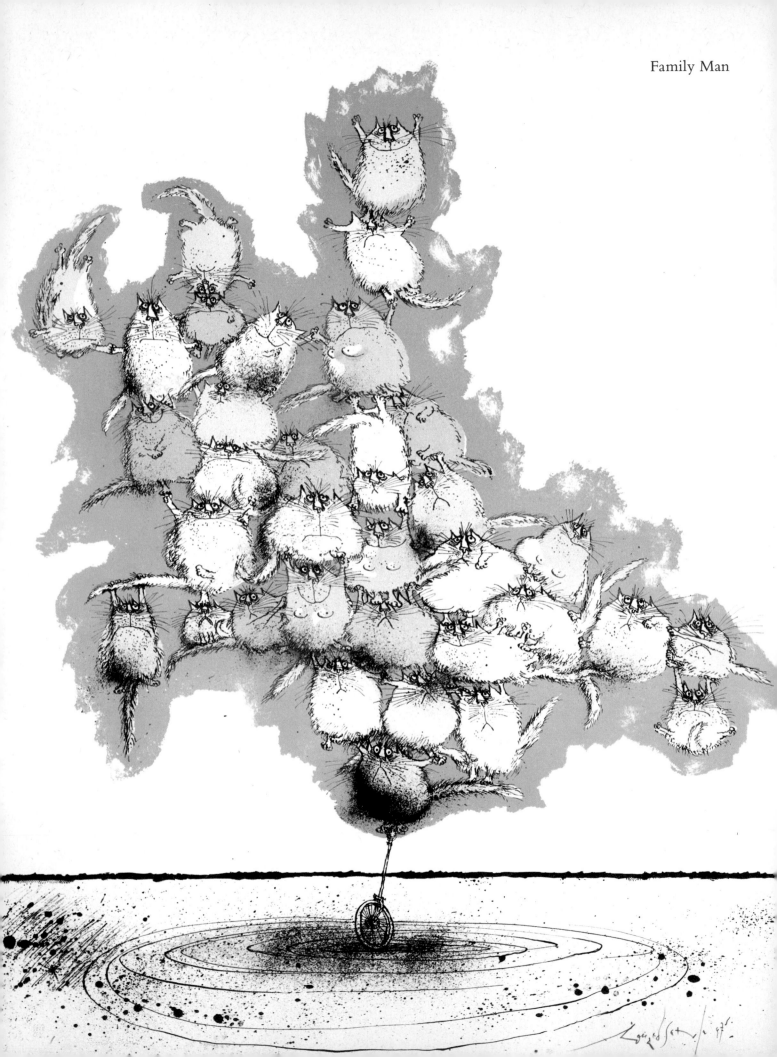

Rat Race

Pussy Posse

Quo Vadis?

Wheeeee!

Big Show

Libra

Five Gold Rings

Irresistible force meets immovable object

The Candidate

The Arrival of the Oracle

Granny Smith

The Long March

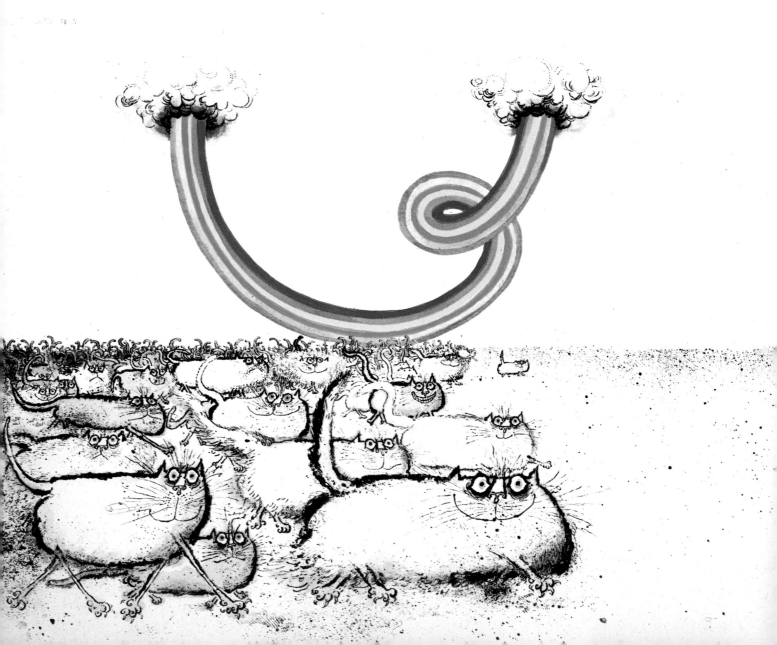

The Coming of the Great Cat God

Displaced Persons

The Owl and the Pussycat

The Stranger

Happy Birthday to you

Congratulations

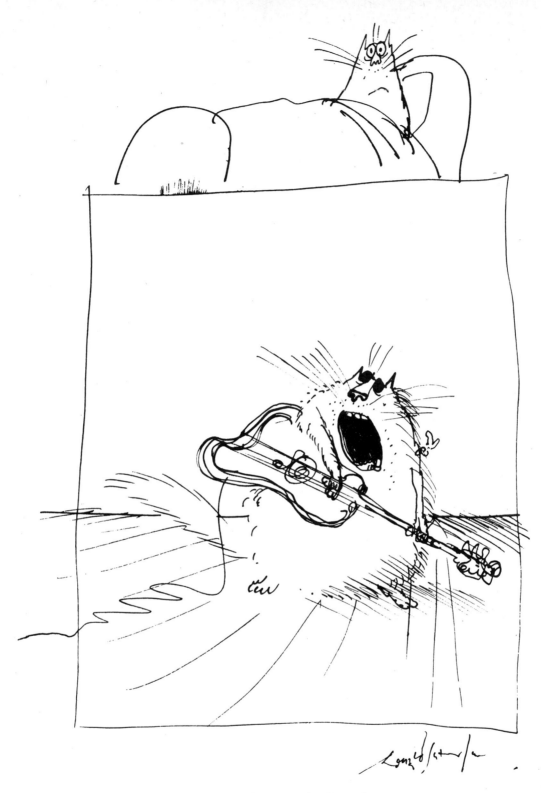

The Sound of Music

Bye Bye Blues

The Good Old Days

Catahari

You bring out the beast in me

The Picnic

The Picnic

Zorro

...

Anticipation

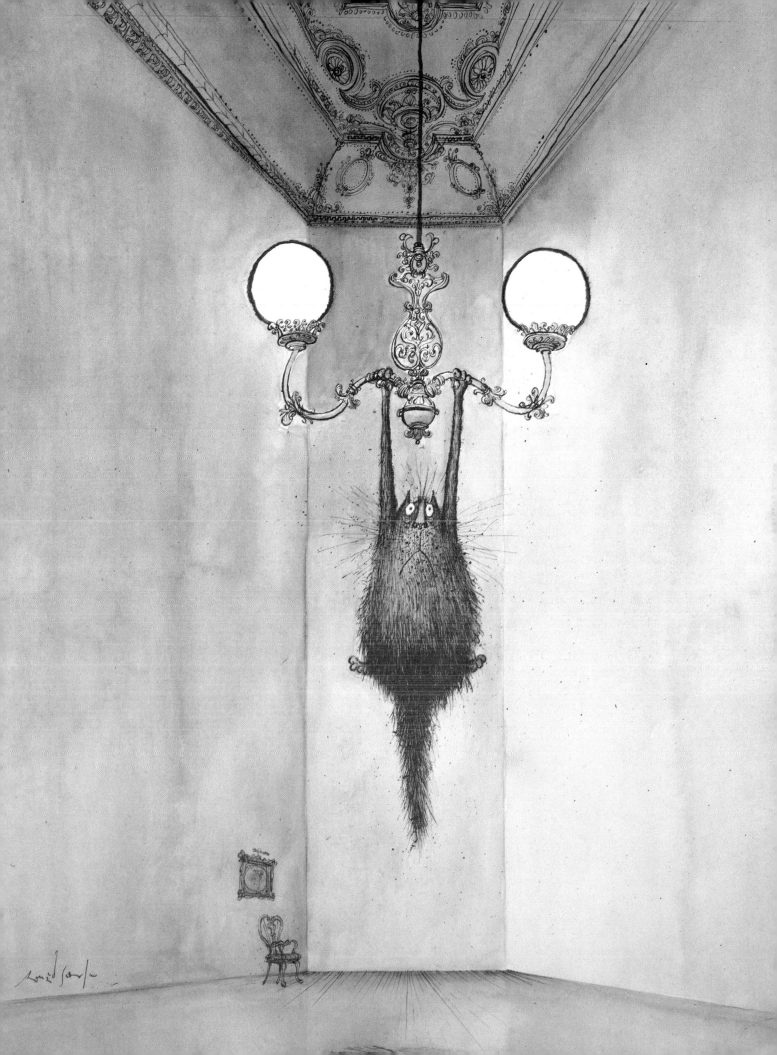

Taking the kitty

I could have danced all night

Darling, this is bigger than both of us . . .

Everybody loves him – the children ADORE him . . .

Catalogue

Nobody wants me

The Frontier

The Encounter

The Exchange

Cats rule OK

The Hoofer

I'm lonely

Memories

L'Apéritif

Dessert

Waterbaby

Nightbird

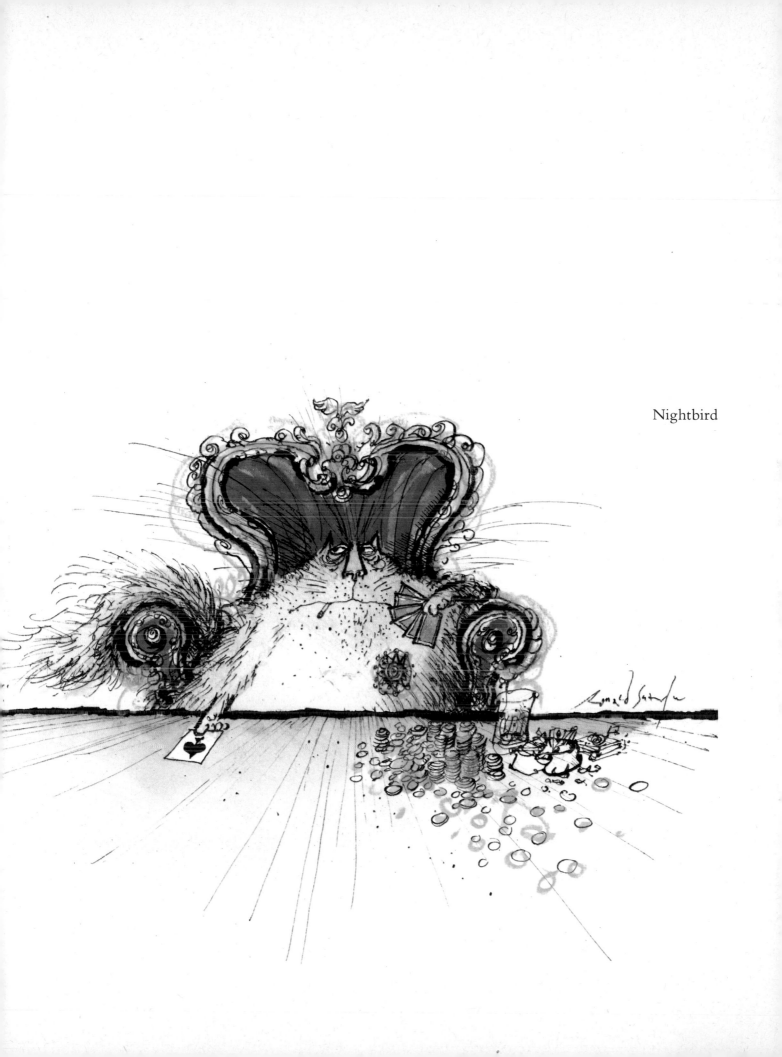

Lady Catterley

Ah yes, I remember it well . . .

The Rendezvous

Hey! There's a cat in the garden . . .

The Champions

Happy Ending

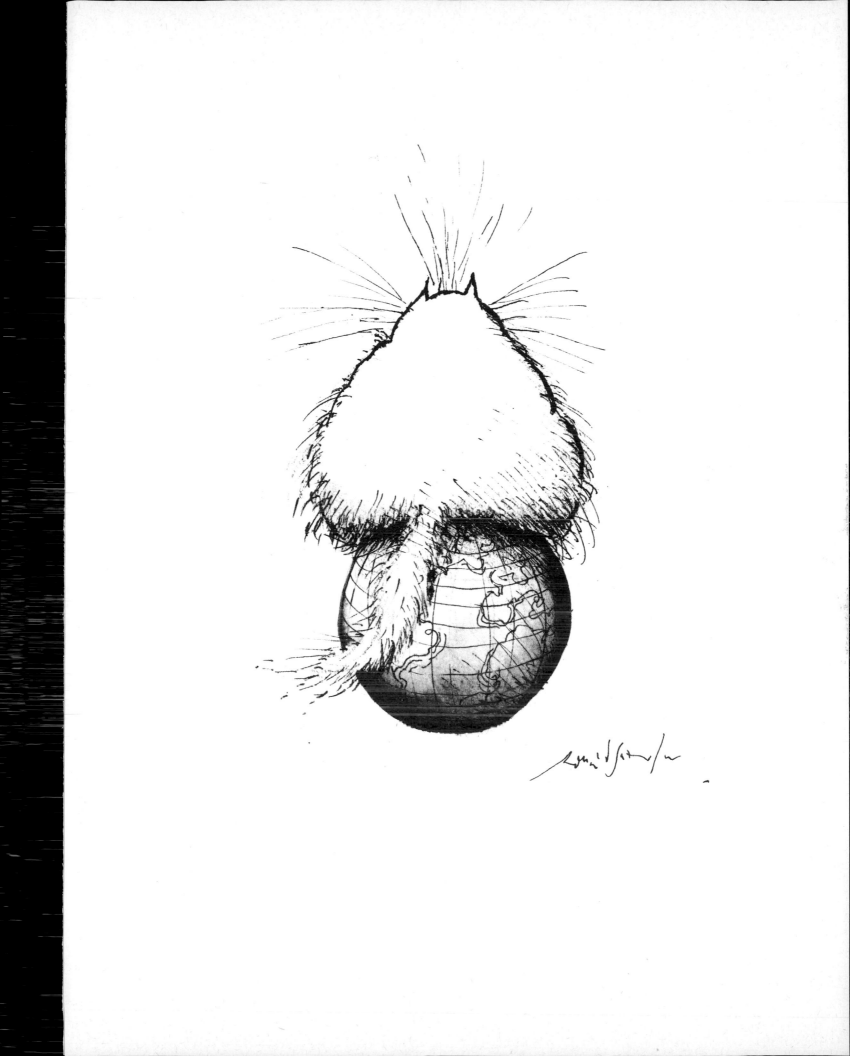